HISTORY OF CRIME AND PUNISHMENT

THE HISTORY OF CRIMINAL LAW

BY DUCHESS HARRIS, JD, PHD
WITH REBECCA ROWELL

Essential Library

An Imprint of Abdo Publishing | abdobooks.com

ABDOBOOKS.COM

Published by Abdo Publishing, a division of ABDO, PO Box 398166, Minneapolis, Minnesota 55439. Copyright © 2020 by Abdo Consulting Group, Inc. International copyrights reserved in all countries. No part of this book may be reproduced in any form without written permission from the publisher. Essential Library™ is a trademark and logo of Abdo Publishing.

Printed in the United States of America, North Mankato, Minnesota.
042019
092019

Interior Photos: Craig Lassig/AP Images, 5; Brian Peterson/Star Tribune/AP Images, 7; Sherburne County Sheriff's Office/AP Images, 9; Jim Mone/AP Images, 13; iStockphoto, 15, 17; Shutterstock Images, 20, 27, 80–81, 83; Rob Carr/AP Images, 24–25; Kevork Djansezian/AP Images, 33; Alan Rogers/Casper Star-Tribune/Trib. com/AP Images, 39; Jessica Hill/AP Images, 41; Sam Gangwer/Orange County Register/AP Images, 44; Hannah Yoon/The Canadian Press/AP Images, 49; Jacqueline Larma/AP Images, 53; Steve Helber/AP Images, 57; Manfred Rutz/ mauritius images GmbH/Alamy, 59; Dan Steinberg/AP Images, 61; Daniel Jedzura/ Shutterstock Images, 63; North Wind Picture Archives, 68; John Bazemore/ AP Images, 71; AP Images, 73; Pablo Martinez Monsivais/AP Images, 77; ESB Professional/Shutterstock Images, 85; RosaIreneBetancourt 7/Alamy, 89; Mike Derer/AP Images, 90; Jae C. Hong/AP Images, 96; Ross D. Franklin/AP Images, 98

Editor: Charly Haley
Series Designer: Dan Peluso

LIBRARY OF CONGRESS CONTROL NUMBER: 2018966052

PUBLISHER'S CATALOGING-IN-PUBLICATION DATA

Names: Harris, Duchess, author | Rowell, Rebecca, author.
Title: The history of criminal law / by Duchess Harris and Rebecca Rowell
Description: Minneapolis, Minnesota: Abdo Publishing, 2020 | Series: History of crime and punishment | Includes online resources and index.
Identifiers: ISBN 9781532119194 (lib. bdg.) | ISBN 9781532173370 (ebook)
Subjects: LCSH: Criminal law--History--Juvenile literature. | Criminal liability-- Law and legislation--Juvenile literature. | Criminology--Juvenile literature. | Crime and criminals--Juvenile literature. | Legal representation of prisoners--Juvenile literature.
Classification: DDC 345.7305--dc23

CONTENTS

CHAPTER ONE

THE JACOB WETTERLING ACT

Jacob Wetterling's parents, Jerry and Patty, hold up a photo of their missing son.

On the night of October 22, 1989, Jacob Wetterling disappeared. The 11-year-old was last seen not far from his home in a rural area near Saint Joseph, Minnesota. Jacob, his little brother, Trevor, and their friend Aaron Larson had biked to a convenience store and rented a movie. On their way back to the Wetterlings' house, a man stopped the boys. He wore a mask and had a gun. He took Jacob.

THE SEARCH BEGINS

A neighbor of the Wetterlings called 911 and reported the abduction. Authorities descended on the site where Jacob was last seen. Dozens of emergency personnel, including firefighters and sheriff's officers, searched the area that night. A helicopter flew overhead, shining a searchlight into the dark fields. People searched late into the night, stopping at about 3:00 a.m. They started again the next morning.

The search for Jacob continued for days. Agents from the Federal Bureau of Investigation (FBI) quickly became involved. On October 25, the FBI released a profile of the suspect: "white man, 25–35 years old, employed in a low-skilled job with a low self-image probably stemming from a physical deformity such as acne or scars."[1] On October 26, Minnesota business leaders offered a reward

Jacob Wetterling was abducted in this area near Saint Joseph, Minnesota.

of $100,000 for the safe return of Jacob within three days. The amount went up to $125,000 the next day with additional funds from Tri-County Crime Stoppers, a nonprofit organization in the Saint Joseph area.

Authorities also released a sketch of the suspect. By November 3, officers had questioned dozens of possible suspects. That day, authorities made a final search of the area where Jacob had been abducted, but they did not find the boy.

The investigation into Jacob's disappearance continued for days, then weeks, and then months. Authorities released more sketches. They also looked for connections between Jacob's case and other reported crimes against local boys his age, including sexual assaults and attempted kidnappings. On January 16, 1990, Jacob's parents, Patty and Jerry Wetterling, announced they would create a foundation to honor their son and to help others affected by childhood kidnapping.

CASE SOLVED

Years passed with little progress in the search for Jacob. Finally, in 2015, investigators had a breakthrough. A local blogger, Joy Baker, had been researching the Wetterling case on her own and posted about similarities between the case and reported attacks in Paynesville, Minnesota. This caught police investigators' attention. Between 1986 and 1988, police in Paynesville had received eight reports of a man attacking young boys. In most of the cases, the man groped the boys and said he would kill them. Paynesville is approximately 30 miles (48 km) from Saint Joseph. The proximity meant the suspect in those cases could be the man who kidnapped Jacob.

During one of the Paynesville attacks, the man dropped his hat. DNA testing revealed the hat belonged to Daniel

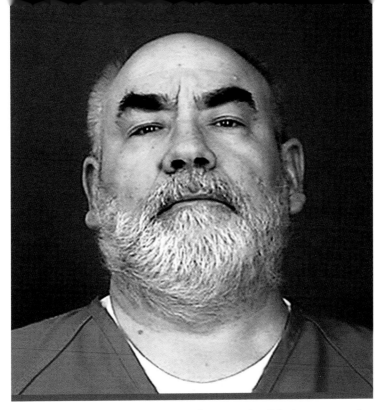
Daniel Heinrich, who killed Jacob Wetterling, was also linked to reports of other young boys being assaulted in Minnesota.

Heinrich. On July 28, 2015, authorities searched Heinrich's home. They found child pornography, which is illegal, and arrested Heinrich. Several weeks later, on August 31, Heinrich led authorities to Jacob's body. After taking Jacob that October night in 1989, Heinrich drove to a field in Paynesville, sexually assaulted Jacob, then shot him. Heinrich buried Jacob not far from where he killed the boy.

A year later, Heinrich returned to the place where he buried Jacob. The grave Heinrich had dug was not very deep. Some of Jacob's red jacket was visible. Heinrich moved the jacket and Jacob's remains to a new grave across the highway. The second grave is where Heinrich led officers. Twenty-seven years after Jacob disappeared, authorities finally found him.

On September 6, 2016, Heinrich confessed in court to abducting, sexually assaulting, and killing Jacob Wetterling. He was sentenced to 20 years in prison for possessing child pornography but not for committing murder. Child pornography possession is a federal crime. Andrew Luger, a federal attorney, explained that authorities made a deal with Heinrich to get him to show law enforcement where he had buried Jacob. The agreement was that, in exchange for this information, Heinrich would be convicted only for child pornography, not for Jacob's murder. Luger told reporters, "He's not getting away with anything. We got the truth. The Wetterling family can bring [Jacob] home."[2]

Patty and Jerry Wetterling agreed to prosecutors making the plea deal. Heinrich would not go to prison for killing their son, but he would go to prison. Patty

PLEA BARGAINING

Often, a defendant takes a plea bargain, also known as a plea deal, instead of letting a jury decide his or her case. Plea bargaining involves the defendant and prosecutors working out a deal in which the defendant pleads guilty to a lesser crime. In cases with multiple charges, the defendant can plead guilty to only some charges in order to get a lighter sentence than would result from conviction by a jury on all charges. The charges to which the defendant does not plead guilty are then dismissed as part of the plea deal.

Wetterling spoke with reporters about the plea, saying, "We need to heal. There's a lot of lessons learned, and there's a lot of work to do to protect all our world's children." She also spoke of her son, focusing on how he lived: "He's taught us all how to live, how to love, how to be fair, how to be kind. He speaks to the world that he knew, that we all believe in. It is a world worth fighting for. His legacy will go on."[3]

NEW FEDERAL LAW

Jacob Wetterling has lived on in different ways. One is through the Jacob Wetterling Resource Center, which educates people with the goal of preventing other children and families from suffering experiences similar to Jacob's. Another part of Jacob's legacy is a federal law that was created in response to his disappearance.

On May 24, 1991, Dave Durenberger, a US senator from Minnesota, proposed legislation to create a national registry of sex offenders. The Jacob Wetterling Crimes Against Children and

PATTY WETTERLING, ADVOCATE

Since her son Jacob's disappearance in October 1989, Patty Wetterling has been an advocate for children and families. In addition to founding the Jacob Wetterling Resource Center in 1990, Wetterling cofounded Team HOPE, a volunteer organization that gives families of missing or exploited children support and resources. Wetterling has also worked for the National Center for Missing and Exploited Children. Closer to home, she worked as the director of sexual violence prevention for the Minnesota Department of Health.

MINNESOTA SEX OFFENDER REGISTRATION

While Jacob Wetterling's disappearance prompted legislation on a national level, it also inspired new laws in his home state. In 1991, Minnesota passed legislation that established the state's first sex offender registry. The law requires all felony sex offenders in the state to register their home address with local law enforcement.

In 1996, the Community Notification Act in Minnesota made local law enforcement responsible for letting area residents know when a sex offender has moved to their community. The law created the Sex Offender Registration Unit, which tracks registered sex offenders in the state. In 2000, a new law changed the name to the Predatory Offender Registration Unit. Every year, the state unit processes approximately 30,000 offender registration updates.[4]

Sexually Violent Offender Registration Act, known simply as the Jacob Wetterling Act, became law in 1994. Before the Jacob Wetterling Act, the United States did not have a nationwide law regarding sex offender registration and notification. The new law did not create a single registry. Rather, it required states to register offenders when they got out of prison. The legislation also established a new class of sex offenders called sexually violent predators and required authorities to verify addresses of these offenders every 90 days. In addition, states had to keep track of offenders for ten years after their release.

The Jacob Wetterling Act is only one example of laws developing or changing in response to a crime. Criminal laws define what acts are considered crimes and how they should be punished. In the case of the Jacob Wetterling Act, a criminal law changed how certain crimes and offenders are

Years after her son disappeared, Patty Wetterling continued to be a vocal advocate for families of missing children.

documented. Criminal law in the United States has a long history, dating back to rules established by the colonists. The nation's system of criminal law is always changing, with these changes often reflecting major events, technological advancements, and other developments.

DISCUSSION STARTERS

- Do you agree that prosecutors should negotiate plea bargains with defendants? Why or why not?
- How might a sex offender registry be helpful? How could it be harmful?
- Why do you think Jacob Wetterling's case was able to prompt changes in state and federal law?

CHAPTER TWO

CRIMINAL LAW
BASICS

Judges interpret and uphold laws when they issue rulings
in court.

The US legal system has two areas of law that address wrongdoing—criminal law and civil law. Criminal law regards illegal acts that are punishable by the government. These include crimes against a person, such as murder. Civil law regards behavior that, while not necessarily illegal, harms a person, a company, or other private entity in some way. One example is breaking a contract.

Sometimes, both criminal and civil cases can result from a single act. For example, if one person assaults another, the person committing the assault can be charged for a crime. In addition, the victim can sue the assailant in civil court. In that civil case, the victim may be seeking money to pay for medical expenses or lost wages as a result of the assault. The victim can start a civil case whether or not there is a criminal case. However, the two cases cannot occur at the same time. The civil case must wait until the criminal case is resolved. If authorities file criminal charges after a civil case has begun, the civil case is put on hold until the criminal case is done.

Criminal and civil law differ in who can file charges or sue and who determines the results of a case. In criminal cases, only the government can press charges, and either a jury or a judge decides the case. In contrast, civil cases begin when

Before a judge or jury makes a decision on a criminal case, the person accused of the crime is allowed to argue for himself or herself in court, usually with help from a lawyer.

a private party sues another private party. A judge, not a jury, usually decides civil cases.

In criminal cases, the prosecution must show "beyond a reasonable doubt" that the defendant, the person accused of the crime, is guilty of that crime.[1] In other words, a guilty verdict must be a logical conclusion based on the facts the prosecution presents. If the jury decides the defendant is guilty and the crime is a felony, or serious crime, the person may be sentenced to time in prison. Punishment may also include paying fines. The punishments in criminal law are intended to protect individuals and society by discouraging people from causing harm to others. Criminal law also holds those who commit crimes accountable for their actions. By doing so, criminal law is meant to bring justice to victims.

There are also laws aimed at protecting people within the criminal justice system and making sure the system treats people fairly. The Fourth Amendment, for example, protects people from unreasonable searches. That includes searches of a person's body, a person's house, and a person's belongings. In order for authorities to conduct a legal search, they must obtain a search warrant approved by a judge.

THE FIFTH AMENDMENT

The Fifth Amendment of the US Constitution addresses five things related to the legal system. First, it requires that a grand jury make a formal Indictment, or accusation, of an individual. Second, double jeopardy is not allowed. That means a person cannot be charged for the same crime twice. Next, the amendment protects a defendant from testifying against himself or herself. The fourth part requires that due process be followed. This is a set of rules for how the government must act. The point is to protect the accused's civil rights. The fifth area involves property. When the government takes private property for public use, it must compensate the owner of the private property.

CRIMINAL LAW ORIGINS

Government officials create laws, including criminal laws. Federal laws apply to the entire country. State laws apply to the individual states and often differ from state to state.

Societies have established criminal laws for centuries. One of the earliest codes of law was the Code of Hammurabi, created by a king who ruled the ancient city of Babylon from 1792 to

1750 BCE. The code followed the philosophy of "an eye for an eye" and detailed severe punishments.[2] Depending on the crime, a person found guilty could have a body part cut off, such as an ear or a tongue.

English common law heavily influenced the history of US criminal law. In England, common law emerged from rulings judges made based on customs and on earlier rulings. For centuries, common law existed as rulings in thousands of court cases. Finally, in the 1500s, English Parliament started creating laws. That moved the country's legal system from common law to a set of written codes that made customs and practices official. Criminal law in the United States has a foundation in English law because of the English colonists who settled in America in the 1600s.

INFRACTION, MISDEMEANOR, FELONY

By law, crimes have different levels of severity. The seriousness of a crime determines the law enforcement and court procedures surrounding the crime. It also determines potential punishments.

Infractions are the least serious. Traffic tickets, such as for speeding, are infractions. Jaywalking is also an infraction in some cities. Usually a police officer gives a person a ticket for committing an infraction. The penalty is a fine. Infractions do not have jail time or probation as punishment. But if a person ignores tickets and does not pay the fines that come with them, the fine may increase, and the court may add penalties. For example, in California, not paying parking tickets can result in the state suspending a person's driver's license. When someone's license is suspended, he or she cannot drive legally until the suspension is done. If a person drives with a suspended license, he or she risks incurring more infractions.

Misdemeanors are more serious than infractions. Someone convicted of a misdemeanor may have to serve

Infractions, such as parking tickets, are punishable by fines but not jail time.

up to one year in jail. Misdemeanor laws vary by state. Ohio has five levels of misdemeanor. From least to most severe, they are: minor, fourth degree, third degree, second degree, and first degree. Each level comes with a limit for jail time and fines. For example, not helping a police officer is a minor misdemeanor in Ohio. It does not carry a possible jail sentence, but it can result in a fine of up to $100. Carrying a gun without a permit is a first-degree misdemeanor in Ohio and can result in up to 180 days in jail and a fine of up to $1,000. Other examples of misdemeanor crimes include trespassing and vandalism.

Felonies are the most serious level of crimes. They can result in prison sentences longer than one year, including life sentences. Felony crimes include arson, burglary, kidnapping, rape, and murder. The federal legal system and many states categorize felonies using letters or numbers. In these systems, class A and level 1 felonies are the most serious, class B and level 2 felonies are less serious, and so on.

Felony categories, like the misdemeanor categories, determine punishment. Each class or level has predetermined guidelines for punishment. New York categorizes felonies from A to E. Categories B through E have two options each: violent or nonviolent. Each category comes with sentencing guidelines. A class E nonviolent felony, such as promoting a suicide attempt, does not result in jail time, but it does have mandatory probation for 16 months to four years. A class A felony, such as first-degree arson, can result in 20 to 25 years in prison. However, if a person has been convicted of a felony in the past, the sentencing minimums and maximums for these and other felonies are often higher. A class A or level 1 felony in one state may be a different class or level in another state. Also, some states do not classify felonies.

PROBATION AND PAROLE

A person convicted of a crime may receive probation or parole as part of his or her sentence. When given probation, the guilty person does not serve time in prison. Instead, he or she is allowed to go free and must maintain good behavior for a specified period. A person on probation usually has

TRIBAL LAW

Native American nations have their own governments and laws that are recognized by the US government. According to the US Bureau of Indian Affairs' website, "Generally, tribal courts have civil jurisdiction over Indians and non-Indians who either reside or do business on federal Indian reservations. They also have criminal jurisdiction over violations of tribal laws committed by tribal members residing or doing business on the reservation." The site also mentions the Indian Tribal Justice Act of 1993, noting that the act "supports tribal courts in becoming, along with federal and state courts, well-established dispensers of justice in Indian Country."[3] In 2010, the Tribal Law and Order Act gave tribal courts more power to prosecute and punish criminals.

to report to a probation officer periodically. A probation agreement often includes requirements such as living in a certain area, having a job, paying restitution, and not drinking alcohol.

An incarcerated convict may be released from prison before his or her sentence expires to serve the rest of the sentence on parole. Unless a sentence has a specific amount of time a person must serve in prison before becoming eligible for parole, a convict is eligible for parole after one-third of his or her sentence. The court system reviews the case and determines whether to grant parole. Like probation, parole comes with terms, such as a requirement to regularly report to a parole officer. Not meeting the terms is a parole violation, which could result in the parolee being returned to prison.

DISCUSSION STARTERS

- Do you think the punishments outlined in criminal law deter crime?
- Do you think it's fair that someone who commits a crime and is charged under criminal law can also be sued under civil law? Why or why not?
- Do you think probation and parole are good or bad? Why?

CONVICTION AND
THE LOSS OF RIGHTS

A felony conviction does not result in only a prison sentence. It may also cause a person to lose some rights. For example, in early 2019, 48 states had laws that took away the right to vote while a person convicted of a felony was in prison. In most of those states, the laws restored the right to vote once incarceration ended. Some states required a waiting period or an application by the person in question before restoring voting rights. In two states, Iowa and Virginia, voting rights could only be restored to convicted felons through special action by the state's governor.[4]

For people whose felony is drug related, traveling abroad may be difficult. Some states take away a drug felon's passport until time is served, including probation or parole. Owning a gun may also be challenging. The process for regaining the right to own a gun varies by state and may include getting a pardon from the governor.

A felony conviction can also affect a person's ability to work and to find reliable housing. It is generally acceptable for an employer to consider a job applicant's criminal history when deciding whether to hire the applicant. In terms of housing and social welfare, people with felony

Activists hold a public demonstration asking lawmakers to restore voting rights for convicted felons. The issue of whether felons should be allowed to vote is debated in many states.

convictions often miss out on assistance such as public housing, food stamps, and other social benefits. That is because people convicted of a felony are not allowed to apply for such support.

VOTING IS A RIGHT

UNLOCK THE VOTE

E-ENFRANCHISEMENT

Our Vo
Our Is
Our V

CHAPTER THREE

CRIMES AGAINST A PERSON

Someone caught committing a crime against a person will usually be arrested and taken to jail.

Crimes against a person is a category under criminal law that includes a variety of offenses, many of which are violent. Crimes in this category also include threat of physical injury and actions done against the victim's will. Examples of crimes against a person include assault, battery, domestic violence, kidnapping, and stalking.

ASSAULT AND BATTERY

Assault and battery often involve hitting or trying to hit someone. The charge can also apply to acting in a threatening way that makes another person feel afraid. Many states have an additional, more serious level of assault and battery—aggravated assault or battery. This is when someone severely hurts another person or attempts to do so, including when someone injures another person using a deadly weapon, such as a gun.

Assault and battery are often mentioned together or interchangeably. Their definitions vary by state, and some states use only one of these terms or use other terms in their criminal laws. Some laws combine assault and battery into one offense because they are related and usually happen together. But often, assault and battery are considered different violations in criminal laws. Generally, assault is an attempt to cause physical harm to another person. Battery involves actually touching another person. The touch must be harmful or offensive, and the person being touched must not have given consent to be touched. A fistfight at a sporting event is an example of battery. One fan might punch another, perhaps because the other person supports the opposing team. Another example is a person spitting on someone. The spit does not cause physical harm, but the spitting could be offensive.

The punishments for being convicted of assault or battery vary by state. Depending on the law, the severity of the crime, and the person's criminal history, the convicted person may have to serve time in jail or pay a fine.

KIDNAPPING

Kidnapping is another personal crime. Kidnapping is taking a person from one place to another without that person's permission. It generally also includes an attempt to harm the person kidnapped or terrorize a

FALSE IMPRISONMENT

False imprisonment is a crime against a person. False imprisonment occurs when someone confines another person, keeping the other person from moving at will. One example is someone robbing a bank who tells everyone to get on the floor. Because the robber has a gun and threatens to shoot people, these people are being held against their will. Police officers can also be guilty of false imprisonment if they hold a person in jail without reason.

third person, such as the victim's spouse. The crime may also involve a ransom demand or an attempt to influence the operation of a government.

Kidnapping has been illegal since colonial times. Kidnapping laws in the United States developed from English common law. Initially, kidnapping was defined as taking a person from one country to another country. Early US kidnapping laws involved moving a person across state lines. State kidnapping laws began removing that requirement in the late 1800s and early 1900s.

The United States passed a law that made interstate kidnapping a federal crime in 1932. The Federal Kidnapping Act, also known as the Lindbergh Law, came about in response to a famous kidnapping. The toddler son of world-renowned pilot Charles A. Lindbergh was kidnapped, taken from his crib. The kidnapper left behind a ransom note and a ladder, which was leaning against the house outside the window of the child's second-floor bedroom. More than two months later, Lindbergh identified a dead child buried in nearby woods as his son.

Two years later, police arrested Bruno Richard Hauptmann for the crime because he had some of the ransom money Lindbergh had paid. But laws were different then than they are now. Kidnapping was not a felony.

So, prosecutors created a felony charge using the laws in place at the time. Stealing a child was not covered under burglary laws—but stealing clothes was. In taking baby Lindbergh, Hauptmann stole the baby's clothing. Prosecutors charged Hauptmann with a death that resulted from the theft of baby Lindbergh's clothing. A jury found Hauptmann guilty of the murder. Hauptmann was executed on April 3, 1936.

In response to this case, the US Congress passed the Lindbergh Law to make kidnapping a federal crime when the victim is taken across state lines. The law also gives federal authorities permission to follow kidnappers across state jurisdictions. A kidnapping conviction usually results in prison time. By federal law, and by some state laws, a person convicted of kidnapping may be punished by life in prison.

AMBER ALERT

In 1996, nine-year-old Amber Hagerman was kidnapped while riding her bike in Arlington, Texas. The kidnappers murdered her. Amber's story prompted the Association of Radio Managers in the Dallas–Fort Worth area to develop the AMBER Alert Program. AMBER Alerts are broadcast across a variety of devices, including radio, television, and cell phones. They provide information about children who have been abducted. The goal is to get as many people as possible looking for the child as quickly as possible. All 50 states, Puerto Rico, the US Virgin Islands, and Washington, DC, use AMBER Alerts. The program's name is short for America's Missing: Broadcast Emergency Response and honors Amber's name.

STALKING

Stalking is another crime against a person that does not always involve physical harm. Stalking is one person excessively pursuing another person. It might involve the stalker physically following the victim on foot or in a car or showing up at the victim's house or job. Stalking can also involve harassing the victim by phone and vandalizing the victim's property. The stalker continues to bother the person; stalking behavior is repeated rather than a one-time occurrence. Stalking is perhaps best known as something that happens to celebrities, but it can involve any person. A stalker may be a stranger, an acquaintance, or, most often, a former romantic partner.

All states and the federal government have laws against stalking. The laws' definitions of stalking vary by how much fear the victim must feel, and some states' laws specify that the victim must fear for his or her life or severe physical harm. Depending on the state and the circumstances, a stalking charge may be a misdemeanor or a felony. In addition to whatever punishment is given, a criminal stalking charge often results in a protective order, also known as a restraining order. These orders, which come from a judge, specify that the stalker must remain a certain distance from the victim. Orders remain in effect for a specific time period. Violating a protective order can have serious consequences in some states, including the stalker having to serve time in jail. So, even if someone does not serve time in jail because he or she was convicted on a misdemeanor stalking charge, that person may serve time for violating a protective order.

One stalking case in California prompted changes to state and federal laws. In 1989, 21-year-old Rebecca Schaeffer starred in the TV sitcom *My Sister Sam*. One of Schaeffer's fans, Robert Bardo, sent her letters and showed up at the television studio where she worked. Bardo also hired a

Robert Bardo was convicted in 1991 for killing actress Rebecca Schaeffer in 1989. Due to the nature of criminal court proceedings, the time between when a person is arrested and convicted can sometimes be years.

private investigator to get Schaeffer's home address from California's Department of Motor Vehicles. After getting the address, Bardo went to Schaeffer's apartment. When Schaeffer opened the door, Bardo shot and killed her.

Bardo was arrested, tried, and convicted of first-degree murder. He was sentenced to life in prison. In response to the Schaeffer case, California lawmakers passed the Driver's Privacy Protection Act in 1994. The law limits who can access the information in state driving records. That same year, the US Congress passed a similar law with the same name as an amendment to the Violent Crime Control and Law Enforcement Act of 1994. A person who purposely violates the federal law will be ordered to pay a fine.

DOMESTIC VIOLENCE

Some victims of stalking experience it as part of another crime: domestic violence. Domestic violence is violent behavior by a person against another person living in the same home or with whom he or she has a relationship. The victim can be a spouse, a child, a romantic or sexual partner, or a roommate. Domestic violence encompasses several types of abuse, including physical abuse, sexual abuse, emotional and psychological abuse, and

HATE CRIMES

A hate crime is violence or threats of violence against someone because of that person's race, ethnicity, national origin, disability, religion, gender, or sexual orientation. Hate crimes were not defined until 1968, when President Lyndon B. Johnson signed the first federal hate crime law. That law protects people in most areas of public life, including while in school, at work, and in public places. In 1996, the Church Arson Prevention Act made vandalizing or destroying religious property a crime. In 2009, new federal legislation broadened the nation's definition of hate crimes to include crimes committed against someone because of the person's disability, gender identity, or sexual orientation. Hate crimes carry more severe penalties than the same crimes committed without the victim being targeted because of race, gender, or other characteristics.

financial control. Each form of abuse is a way for the abuser to control the victim.

State laws vary on domestic abuse, including varied definitions of the crime. Some state criminal laws specify only physical abuse. Some acknowledge other types of abuse. Hawaii's definition includes actual physical harm, threatened physical harm, psychological abuse, and property damage. A first offense results in mandatory jail time of at least 48 hours. If a second offense occurs within one year of the first conviction, the person must serve at least 30 days in jail and take part in a counseling program. If the person commits a third offense within two years of the second conviction, the person is charged with a felony. A class C felony conviction carries up to five years in prison and a fine of up to $10,000.

Domestic violence was illegal in all states by 1920. But this did not necessarily mean police got involved. Often, people thought of domestic abuse situations as personal or family matters. This view began to change in the 1970s, when the legal system began to treat domestic violence as a serious offense.

In 1984, the US attorney general, the country's chief legal adviser, recommended that arrest be made the standard practice when police respond to calls about domestic violence. The recommendation was a response to a study that found that arrest was more effective in preventing additional acts of domestic violence than other actions, such as mediation. Lawsuits also played a role in changing the way police officers addressed domestic violence. Some abused women claimed negligence by their local police. In 1984, Tracy Thurman, who was nearly killed by her husband, won her case against the police department in Torrington, Connecticut. She sued the police department because its policies for domestic violence calls included not intervening and not arresting. Thurman was awarded $1.9 million.[1]

In 1994, the US Congress passed the Violence Against Women Act (VAWA). The law made some forms of domestic violence federal crimes, including interstate stalking and violating a protective order. In 2013, the Violence Against Women Act was reauthorized with updates to improve efforts against domestic violence and rape. These included broadening the power of Native American governments. Specifically, according to the US Department of Justice:

> Tribes are able to exercise their sovereign power to investigate, prosecute, convict, and sentence both Indians and non-Indians who assault Indian spouses or dating partners or violate a protection order in Indian country. VAWA 2013 also clarifies tribes' sovereign power to issue and enforce civil protection orders against Indians and non-Indians.[2]

The 2013 reauthorization also increased efforts to provide education about domestic violence and support for victims. For crimes, the law updated stalking to include electronic communications, such as harassment over texting or social media.

DISCUSSION STARTERS

- Were there any criminal laws in this chapter that surprised you? What about it was surprising?
- What do you think about the ways the laws described in this chapter developed over time?
- What are your thoughts about hate crime laws? Are they important? Will they deter hate crimes?

CHAPTER FOUR

MURDER AND MANSLAUGHTER

Law enforcement officers arrive at the scene of a reported homicide.

Homicide is any instance in which a person takes another person's life. Not all homicides are criminal. Examples of noncriminal homicide include deaths as a result of enforcing the death penalty and homicides committed in self-defense. But when homicides are deemed criminal, they're called murder or manslaughter. Because they result in death, murders are the most severe of violent crimes. In 2016, murders accounted for 1.4 percent of the nation's 1.2 million violent crimes.[1]

LEVELS OF MURDER

Like other crimes, murder has levels of legal severity. First-degree murder is the most severe. These killings are usually premeditated, or planned. They are intentional. Second-degree murder, like first-degree murder, is also usually intentional. However, it is not premeditated.

Next are voluntary and involuntary manslaughter. The legal definitions of these crimes vary by state. All state laws define these crimes as a person killing another person; the factor that varies is the killer's state of mind. Voluntary manslaughter is usually a killing that occurs without thought, such as during a passionate argument. Unlike second-degree murder, in which the killer is deemed to have a full

Police investigate the scene of a murder in Connecticut.

understanding of his or her actions, voluntary manslaughter involves a circumstance under which a reasonable person is deemed to have become emotionally disturbed or prompted by impulse. Manslaughter is committed in the heat of the moment. By contrast, involuntary manslaughter is unintentional. It occurs as a result of being reckless or neglectful, such as by driving while intoxicated.

THE DEATH PENALTY

Under federal law, first-degree murder and second-degree murder are punishable by life in prison. However, people convicted of first-degree murder can also receive the death penalty. Each year, the criminal justice system put convicts to death as punishment for their crimes. Twenty-three convicts were executed in 2017. As of July 1, 2018, more than 2,700 convicted felons were awaiting execution.[2] Under federal law, the death penalty can be used as punishment for 41 crimes, including murder, espionage, and treason. By state laws, the death penalty is usually only used to punish murderers.

In early American history, criminals were put to death for many more crimes, including arson, counterfeiting, rape, robbery, and horse theft. The earliest recorded execution in the American colonies took place in 1608 in the Virginia colony. The person executed, George Kendall, had been convicted of spying for Spain. Four years later, Virginia's governor established a set of laws that made the death penalty the punishment for a variety of crimes. Some of the offenses were minor, including killing chickens and stealing grapes. Other colonies established their own laws. In 1665, the New York colony made hitting one's parent punishable by death.

MENS REA

Mens rea is a feature of criminal law. The phrase *mens rea* is Latin for "guilty mind."[3] This refers to a defendant's state of mind when committing a crime. The point of mens rea is to help the criminal justice system determine whether a person intended to commit the crime for which he or she is accused. Laws have not always been clear about mens rea. Over time, however, laws have addressed intent with words such as *knowingly*, *purposely*, *recklessly*, and *negligently*.

Around the time of the American Revolutionary War (1775–1783), the number of crimes punishable by the death penalty decreased dramatically. States also began taking other measures regarding the death penalty. In 1834, Pennsylvania became the first state to stop public executions. Over the years, states have abolished and reinstated the death penalty, as has the federal government. The US Supreme Court has made several rulings on the death penalty. A 2008 ruling established that the death penalty could not be used as punishment for a crime against a person in which the victim lived. The case in question regarded the rape of a girl in Louisiana, a state that had made rape punishable by death in 1995. The Supreme Court ruled 5–4 that Louisiana could not execute the rapist, Patrick Kennedy, because he did not kill or intend to kill the victim. As of 2018, the death penalty was legal in 30 states.[4]

VEHICULAR HOMICIDE

Some laws address a specific form of homicide. Vehicular homicide, which is also called vehicular manslaughter, is homicide caused by someone driving a car. It is reckless and negligent, not intentional. In these cases, the vehicle is considered a weapon.

If someone is killed in a car accident, depending on the circumstances, it may be considered vehicular homicide.

In 1910, New York became the first state to make driving while intoxicated a crime. Driving while intoxicated often results in car accidents that cause injury and death. The criminal charge of vehicular manslaughter developed later in response to a high number of deaths caused by car accidents. Vehicular homicide has different levels. Ordinary negligence is, according to the legal website Justia, "When the driver fails to act with the same level of care that a reasonable person would under the circumstances."[5] Gross negligence is a greater crime and may include driving the wrong way on a street or at very high speeds in excess of the speed limit. Punishment depends on the details of the crime and the state's laws regarding vehicular homicide. Ordinary negligence may result in a misdemeanor, and gross negligence may result in a felony.

FELONY MURDER

In addition to charging murder as a felony, some states define and prosecute a separate crime called felony murder. This is a killing that occurs while committing a separate felony. For example, California has a felony murder law that holds people responsible for murder by association. Shawn Khalifa was sentenced to 25 years to life in prison after being convicted under that law. On January 27, 2004, Khalifa was one of four teenagers who broke into the house of his elderly neighbor. The teens were looking for money. Khalifa, who was 15, stood guard at the back door. When he stepped into the kitchen and took some candy, Khalifa saw the man who owned the house, 77-year-old Hubert Love, seriously injured. Khalifa ran outside. The teens got caught, and Love died. Under California's felony murder law, Khalifa was tried and convicted of first-degree murder.

In 2018, Nancy Skinner, a state senator in California, introduced a bill to change the state's felony murder law.

She proposed this change because the felony murder law was affecting women and young black and Latino men more than other people. In 2018, three California groups supporting criminal justice reform surveyed 1,000 inmates in California prisons and found that 72 percent of women serving life sentences for murder did not do the killing themselves. In addition, the average age of those convicted for felony murder was 20.[6] Skinner said, "They had bad judgment, but they didn't commit a murder—and when I understood this, I knew we had to fix that."[7]

On September 30, 2018, California governor Jerry Brown signed the bill into law. It took effect on January 1, 2019. The new law limits the acts that can be prosecuted as felony murder. Instead of an accused person simply being part of the felony being committed when the person was murdered, the new law states the person must have played a direct part in the murder or have been "a major participant in the underlying felony and acted with reckless indifference to human life."[8] The new law also makes it possible for people serving time for felony murder to request resentencing, meaning receiving a new sentence based on the new law. Those who support this new law believe 400 to 800 people currently incarcerated for felony murder could

ONE ACTION, TWO COURT CASES

On December 22, 1984, Bernhard Goetz got onto a subway train in New York City. Goetz was carrying a handgun, which he started doing after he was assaulted by three teenagers at a subway station in 1981. Goetz did not have a permit to carry the gun.

Four teenagers were also on the subway car. The teens asked Goetz for $5. When Goetz said no, one of the teens demanded, "Give me your money."[11] Expecting the worst, Goetz responded by shooting his gun. He wounded all four teens. Goetz ran away when the train made its next stop. Eight days later, he turned himself in to authorities. In 1987, the jury in his criminal trial found Goetz not guilty of attempted murder, which is a felony, and guilty of possessing a firearm illegally, a misdemeanor. Goetz spent less than a year behind bars.

However, one of the teens who was shot, Darrell Cabey, later sued Goetz in civil court. The wound paralyzed Cabey. In 1996, Cabey won the case and was awarded $43 million to be paid by Goetz. Goetz immediately filed for bankruptcy and did not pay.

apply for resentencing.[9] Opponents were concerned that the law would let people who have done wrong go free without making them responsible for their actions. Skinner said in response to the signing that the bill was "a fair and reasonable fix to California's unjust felony murder rule."[10]

DISCUSSION STARTERS

- Why aren't all homicides criminal? Do you think they should be?
- Do you agree with the death penalty? Why or why not?
- Do you think it's important to consider mens rea, or a suspect's intent, when investigating a crime? Why or why not?

CHAPTER FIVE

SEX CRIMES

Activists work to raise awareness about the severity and
prevalence of sex crimes.

Criminal laws on sex crimes cover a variety of offenses. Most of these crimes involve illegal, forced sexual behavior by one person against another, such as rape and sexual assault. However, some acts without a direct victim, such as possession of child pornography, are also considered sex crimes.

RAPE

Rape is sexual intercourse that is not consensual. Years ago, according to the legal website FindLaw, "Common law defined rape as unlawful intercourse by a man against a woman who is not his wife by force or threat and against her will."[1] Over time, the definition changed. Today, laws have a broader definition that does not include requirements for marriage, gender, or physical force. A critical factor is the victim's lack of consent. Consent is a person's willing agreement to engage in a sexual act. For example, a person intoxicated by alcohol or drugs may be unable to consent.

According to the FBI, in 2016, almost 8 percent of violent crime was rape.[2] Rape can occur between people who are strangers. It can also occur between people who know each other, including when the offender and victim are dating. Spousal rape, also known as marital rape, occurs when the offender and victim are married. Statutory rape involves sexual intercourse between an adult and a minor. Even if the minor agrees to having sex, that person, as a minor, cannot legally give consent. Sexual penetration of some form needs to have taken place to convict a person of rape. And each occurrence of penetration can result in a separate criminal charge.

Rape laws carry severe criminal penalties, although the laws vary by state. For example, New York state law defines three degrees of rape, all of which are felonies. Punishments for these crimes range from a prison sentence of up to four years and fines of up to $5,000 for third-degree rape to between five and 25 years in prison and fines of up to $5,000

SPOUSAL RAPE

Historically, England's laws long held that marital rape was impossible. That idea carried over to American common law. Under these laws, marriage was consent. In 1857, a case in Massachusetts became the first in the United States to acknowledge the idea of marriage being consent under law.

Initially, state laws purposely excluded spouses in their definitions of rape. That began to change in the 1970s. In 1976, Nebraska became the first state to end its marital exception for rape, making spousal rape illegal. Three years later, a case in Salem, Massachusetts, seemed to be a national turning point. A man who was drunk charged into the house he used to share with his wife and raped her. The two were separated and in the process of divorcing. The man's actions were considered a home invasion and violent. He was convicted of rape in the first known conviction of spousal rape in the United States. By 1983, 17 states had changed their laws to include spousal rape. By 1993, all 50 states had removed the marital rape exception from their laws.

for first-degree rape. New York's criminal laws also specify statutes of limitations. This is a time limit for filing charges against someone for a crime. As of early 2019, the statutes of limitations in New York for second- and third-degree rape were both five years. There was no statute of limitations for first-degree rape in the state.

Statutes of limitations vary by state, including those for rape. Victims of rape or sexual assault in Montana have ten years to report the crime, and those in Nevada have 20 years. Many people have criticized statutes of limitations for rape cases, and, as a result, some states have reconsidered their laws. For example, California ended its statute of limitations for many sex crimes in September 2016 as a result of a case involving comedian Bill Cosby. Decades after they were assaulted by the celebrity, dozens of women reported their experiences to authorities. The standard limit for felony sexual offenses had been ten years.

In the late 2010s, people began advocating for the change or removal of statutes of limitations on sex crimes. For example, in 2017, Illinois removed its statute of limitations for three sex crimes, including aggravated sexual abuse against children. Lisa Madigan, Illinois's attorney general at that time, told *PBS NewsHour*:

Police officers escort comedian Bill Cosby to a Pennsylvania prison, where he was sentenced to serve three to ten years for sexual assault.

> *Tragically, there are millions of people whose childhoods are*
>
> *tarnished by sexual assault and sexual abuse. For decades they*
>
> *struggle to come to terms with the terrible impacts these crimes*
>
> *have on their lives—including the troubling fact that very few of*
>
> *the perpetrators are held accountable.*[3]

Sexual assault victims often struggle with statutes of limitations because, as the Cosby case shows, it can take years for victims to feel comfortable coming forward and discussing the abuse that they've suffered. It takes time for people to cope with the emotional trauma of rape. Additionally, some victims choose not to speak out right away because they fear retaliation, especially if the perpetrator is in a position of power or has made a threat. Others feel they may not be believed if they come forward. And still others feel as if they each must be the only victim, so they choose to keep their stories to themselves.

In many states, legislators have changed laws to reflect what seems to be a better understanding of victims. As of January 2019, seven states had eliminated their statutes of limitations for all felony sex crimes. Those states were Kentucky, Maryland, North Carolina, South Carolina, Virginia, West Virginia, and Wyoming.[4]

REVISED RAPE DEFINITION

In 2012, the US Department of Justice (DOJ) revised its definition of rape for the Uniform Crime Reporting (UCR) Program. Through the UCR, the FBI gathers crime statistics. Since 1927, UCR's definition of forcible rape included only a man acting against a woman and involving his penis in her vagina. The 2012 change broadened the definition of rape: "The penetration, no matter how slight, of the vagina or anus with any body part or object, or oral penetration by a sex organ of another person, without the consent of the victim."[5] This definition was a first for the DOJ in acknowledging that rape is genderless and can include different sexual acts. The new definition is used for gathering data on sex crimes. The broadened language was intended to improve accuracy.

SEXUAL ASSAULT

In criminal law, sexual assault is a broader category than rape. This category, which is sometimes called sexual abuse, includes an array of nonconsensual sex-related behaviors that are illegal. Sexual assault includes touching a person sexually without his or her consent. Exposing oneself to a person without consent and voyeurism, or spying on someone, such as through a bedroom window, are also forms of sexual assault.

Federal legal code includes a law against sexual abuse. People convicted of the crime can be sentenced to life in prison. All 50 states ban sexual assault. They classify these crimes similarly, for the most part. But many states use slightly different definitions of rape and sexual assault in their criminal laws, and some don't even use those terms as criminal charges. For example, Minnesota's criminal code refers to all levels of rape and sexual assault as *criminal sexual conduct*. Rape is charged as first-degree criminal sexual conduct. Some states create individual laws for different sexual acts while others do not.

CHILD PORNOGRAPHY

Another type of sex crime is child pornography. Creating, possessing, distributing, and selling sexual images of people younger than 18 is illegal under federal and state laws. In 1977, the Protection of Children against Sexual Exploitation

Act became the first federal law to specifically address child pornography, making filming or photographing children performing sexual acts illegal. The states soon followed, creating their own laws to criminalize child pornography.

Over the years, Congress has added legislation to expand the acts that are defined as criminal. In 1988, the Child Protection and Obscenity Enforcement Act made transmitting, distributing, or receiving child pornography using a computer illegal. Today, federal child pornography legislation outlaws selling or buying children, sexual exploitation of minors, and material containing child pornography, which includes using computers to transmit child pornography.

Child pornography crimes carry severe penalties. A first-time offender convicted of creating child pornography can be sentenced to 15 to 30 years in prison. Texas criminal law has four classes of child pornography, including class A misdemeanor and third-, second-, and first-degree felonies. The penalties for those crimes range from a fine of up to $4,000 and up to one year in jail to a fine of up to $10,000 and five years to life in prison.

Many people convicted of sex crimes must register as sex offenders. Various pieces of legislation have created federal

Sex offender registry information from all states is accessible online.

and state sex offender registries. In addition, some states limit where convicted sex offenders can live, such as not allowing them to live within a certain distance of schools.

DISCUSSION STARTERS

- What do you think about statutes of limitations? Should they be discarded? Explain.
- This chapter describes legal definitions of sex crimes that have changed over time. What do you think of these changes? Are there other laws described that you think need to change?
- Do you think the laws described in this chapter effectively help victims of sexual assault? Explain.

CHAPTER SIX

PROPERTY CRIMES

Theft, such as shoplifting, is a property crime.

n 2016, Americans reported almost eight million property crimes to authorities.[1] There are many different types of property crimes. Some property crimes include various forms of theft, such as shoplifting, burglary, and robbery. Shoplifting is intentionally taking goods from a store without paying for them. Burglary involves illegally entering someone's property (such as their home or business) with the intention to steal. Burglary does not require a victim to be present when the crime is happening, but robbery does. In a robbery, one person takes something from another person by using violence or threatening harm. An example is someone forcing employees at a bank to hand over cash by threatening to shoot them.

Other crimes involve damaging or destroying property. Arson is when someone intentionally sets a building or other structure or a forest on fire. Vandalism involves damaging property. Egging someone's house or car is vandalism.

Property crimes vary in their severity, ranging from misdemeanor to felony. The level of severity is related to factors such as the value of what was stolen, the use of force, and physical harm or the potential for physical harm. Punishments range from fines to prison time.

ARSON

Arson can involve burning one's own property or another person's property. Some people set their own property on fire in an attempt to get money from their insurance company. This act results in two crimes: arson and insurance fraud. Arson can also cause physical harm to others or even death. In most cases, arson is a felony.

Arson laws exist at the state and federal levels. In 1996, the federal Church Arson Prevention Act became law. The law emerged in response to a string of 145 arsons at African American churches between 1995 and 1996.[2] The law increased the maximum sentence for a church arson from

Firefighters work to extinguish fires set on multiple cars in a string of arson attacks in Los Angeles, California, in 2012.

10 years to 20. In addition, President Bill Clinton formed the National Church Arson Task Force (NCATF). Between January 1, 1995, and August 15, 2000, the NCATF investigated 945 church arsons or bombings. The organization arrested 431 suspects related to 342 of the crimes.[3]

In an example of arson laws changing at the state level, Michigan made its arson laws tougher in 2013. Among the changes was a maximum sentence of life in prison for first-degree arson. Michigan's government also established that this category of arson includes any arson that hurts someone physically and any arson of a multifamily building, regardless of injuries. In addition to being incarcerated, people convicted of first-degree arson in Michigan can be fined up to $20,000. This fine also applies to arson for insurance fraud.

Michigan legislators created the 2013 arson law to reflect a change in views about arson. Officials recognized the human toll of the crime. In 2011, state police officers responded to more than 10,000 arsons or suspicious fires that resulted in 67 deaths and more than 130 injuries. Amy Dehner, legislative liaison for the Michigan State Police, said of arson, "A lot of people think it's just a property crime. It's not. It's a violent crime."[4]

THEFT

Of the eight million property crimes reported in 2016, approximately 71 percent were theft.[5] Theft, known in some state laws as larceny, is taking someone else's property permanently without permission to do so and without plans to give the stolen items back. Many states have degrees, or levels, of theft. Some states specify two levels—petty theft and grand theft. Laws describe a dollar value that serves as the dividing line between the two levels. Petty theft involves property valued at less than the set dollar amount, and grand theft involves property valued at more than that amount.

Stealing an expensive item, such as a car, would result in a more severe punishment than a lower level of theft.

In California, for example, the dividing line is $400. If the stolen property is valued at less than $400, the charge is petty theft. If the value is $400 or more, the charge is grand theft. Both can result in a misdemeanor charge. A misdemeanor carries three years of probation and up to six months in a jail, a fine of $1,000, or both jail time and fine. Grand theft can also result in a felony charge when the stolen property has a high value. The punishment for a felony is a prison sentence of up to three years.

Some states break down petty and grand theft further. For example, Florida has two levels of petty theft and three levels of grand theft. As the value of the stolen property increases, so does the punishment. Florida's lowest level of theft is second-degree petty theft. The value of the property is less than $100. The maximum punishment is 60 days in jail and a fine of $500. First-degree grand theft is the highest level. The stolen property has a value of at least $100,000. The maximum punishment is 30 years in prison and a fine of up to $10,000. Some states have a separate theft category for vehicles, often called grand theft auto.

In the 2000s and 2010s, several states changed their laws to increase the dollar value required for a theft to be a felony. Since 2000, 37 states have adjusted their theft felony minimums, partly to decrease the number of people who go to prison for theft.[6] Lawmakers wanted people convicted of serious crimes, rather than relatively minor thefts, to go to prison.

People who opposed such changes expressed concern that increasing the felony threshold might result in more property crime. With the cutoff amount being higher, some people might be more inclined to steal knowing the risk for felony had decreased. A Pew Charitable Trusts study found that these worries did not materialize. Pew compared felony theft in the 30 states that increased their felony limits between the years 2000 and 2012 with the 20 states that did not raise their limits. Felony rates decreased nationwide, with

MIRANDA RIGHTS

When being arrested for any crime, a person has rights. Some of these are detailed in what are known as Miranda rights. Miranda rights developed in response to the 1966 US Supreme Court case *Miranda v. Arizona*. In March 1963, police in Phoenix, Arizona, arrested Ernesto Miranda for abducting and raping an 18-year-old woman. Police interrogated Miranda. Not knowing he did not have to speak with police, Miranda confessed to the crime and later recanted, or took it back. Miranda was convicted and sent to prison. The American Civil Liberties Union issued an appeal, saying police forced the false confession. The Supreme Court ruled in Miranda's favor and overturned his conviction. The court's decision created what became known as Miranda rights, establishing that a person questioned by police must be informed of his or her right to talk to a lawyer.

The language of Miranda rights is familiar to many people because of its frequent use in police dramas: "You have the right to remain silent. Anything you say can and will be used against you in a court of law. You have the right to an attorney. If you cannot afford an attorney, one will be provided for you. Do you understand the rights I have just read to you? With these rights in mind, do you wish to speak to me?"[7]

ENVIRONMENTAL LAW

Some federal laws address environmental issues, such as air and water quality. The Environmental Protection Agency (EPA) enforces these laws. When severe violations occur, the EPA can file criminal charges. Punishments for these crimes can include fines and prison time. The EPA can also hold violators responsible for cleaning up the environment. For example, in a 2017 case regarding a violation of the Clean Air Act, construction company Aireko was fined $1.5 million. Aireko had removed asbestos from an office building in an illegal way that caused people to be exposed to the hazardous mineral. Asbestos, a mineral that has been used as fire-resistant insulation, causes lung problems and can cause cancer. Aireko's sentence included $172,020 for medical exams for approximately 450 people exposed to the asbestos. Edgardo Albino, Aireko's vice president, also received an individual sentence. He pleaded guilty to not notifying the National Response Center about the asbestos, which is required by federal law. His sentence was a fine of $15,000 and three years of probation.

a drop of 39 percent between 1998 and 2015. The changes to felony theft minimums did not affect the rate. When looking specifically at the 30 states with increased limits, Pew found that 24 of them had lower property crime rates in 2015, the last year of the data examined, than they had in the year their new legislation went into effect.[8]

FRAUD AND FINANCIAL CRIMES

A subset of theft laws includes fraud and financial crimes, such as bribery, identity theft, and tax evasion. Bribery is illegally giving or taking money or a favor in exchange for influencing a decision. For example, a business leader might give money to a city leader to win a contract to do work for the city. Identity theft is illegally pretending to be someone else, such as getting a credit card in another person's name and then using it and leaving the person to pay for the debt. Tax evasion is failing to pay one's taxes as required by law.

Tax evasion and other financial crimes are often called white-collar crimes. The term *white-collar crime* refers to crimes often committed by people who have high-level or corporate jobs, known as white-collar jobs. In addition to tax evasion, the most common white-collar crimes are embezzlement, fraud, and money laundering. Embezzlement is when someone who is given responsibility for money or property, such as at his or her job, takes that money or property for personal use. It is a form of stealing. Money laundering is transferring money obtained through criminal activities into legal entities, such as banks, to hide how the money was obtained illegally. The FBI estimates that white-collar crime costs the country more than $300 billion every year.[9]

HISTORY OF AMERICAN WHITE-COLLAR CRIME

In the United States, white-collar crime became common in the 1800s after the Industrial Revolution. The economy was changing and growing. Some companies did better than others and wiped out the competition. Eventually, some

Political cartoons in the late 1800s depicted monopolies as greedy and powerful, crushing business competition and political reform efforts.

companies became monopolies, which means they became the only business in their industry. That allowed them to raise prices. Greedy and eager to make as much money as possible, monopolies charged very high prices. This was legal at the time, but many Americans thought it should be against the law.

In 1890, the Sherman Antitrust Act, the first white-collar crime law, made monopolies illegal in the United States. Since then, the US government has created a variety of laws defining white-collar crime, including mail fraud, tax fraud, and securities fraud. Penalties vary and include fines, home detention, and prison sentences. States have also enacted laws regarding white-collar crime.

In 2009, Bernie Madoff pleaded guilty to multiple white-collar crimes, including 11 felony fraud crimes. Posing as a financial adviser, Madoff had conned people out of their money by saying he would invest it for them. The crimes Madoff admitted to committing included investment adviser fraud, mail fraud, and theft from an employee benefit plan. Madoff told authorities he lost $50 billion people had given him to invest. Madoff got the maximum sentence for his crimes and is serving a 150-year prison sentence.

DISCUSSION STARTERS

- What do you think about the changes to arson laws described in this chapter? How was the nature of that crime considered by lawmakers?
- Do think increasing the dollar value for a felony theft is a good idea or a bad idea? Explain.
- Are Miranda rights important? Why or why not?

CHAPTER SEVEN

DRUG CRIMES

When police arrest a person on suspicion of drug crimes, officers confiscate any drugs they can find and package these drugs as evidence.

According to the FBI, authorities made 1.57 million arrests for drug crimes nationwide in 2016, which averages out to one arrest every 20 seconds.[1] The number of arrests was more than 5 percent higher than it had been in 2015. The number is also more than three times greater than the total number of arrests for all violent crimes that year. Many advocates attribute the high number of drug arrests in the United States to the federal War on Drugs campaign that started decades ago. Maria McFarland Sánchez-Moreno is the executive director of Drug Policy Alliance, a nonprofit organization working to end the War on Drugs. "Criminalizing drug use has devastated families across the US, particularly in communities of color, and for no good reason," Sánchez-Moreno said. "Far from helping people who are struggling with addiction, the threat of arrest often keeps them from accessing health services and increases the risk of overdose or other harms."[2]

HISTORY OF THE WAR ON DRUGS

People in the United States have used drugs for medical treatment and personal recreation for as long as the country has existed. States began passing laws to control or ban drugs in the 1800s. The first federal drug-related law

Officers in 1925 examine a large amount of illegal smoking opium they seized from a ship near New York City.

emerged in 1890, but it did not ban any substances. Rather, the law assessed taxes on two drugs, morphine and opium. In 1909, the Smoking Opium Exclusion Act, which banned nonmedical possession and use of opium, became the first federal law banning a drug for nonmedical use. In 1914, the Harrison Act affected opiates and cocaine, regulating and taxing their importation, production, and distribution. In 1937, the Marihuana Tax Act passed, taxing the sale of marijuana. The maximum punishment under that law was a $2,000 fine and five years in prison for not paying the tax.

In 1951, Congress passed the first federal mandatory minimum-sentencing laws for drug crimes. Many states have mandatory minimum laws, which require judges to give minimum sentences for particular crimes, regardless of the circumstances of the case. According to the Criminal Justice

Policy Foundation, "These laws take away from a judge the traditional and proper authority to account for the actual circumstances of the crime and the characteristics of the individual defendant when imposing a sentence."[3] Under these first federal mandatory minimum laws, first-time possession of marijuana, cocaine, or heroin garnered at least two years in prison. The maximum sentence was five years. The required minimum sentence for trafficking, or distributing, drugs was five years.

Recreational drug use in the United States increased during the 1960s. By 1969, almost 50 percent of Americans believed drugs were a major problem.[4] In 1970, President Richard Nixon signed the Controlled Substances Act into law. The law regulates many drugs, placing them in five categories, called schedules. The schedules rank the substances based on their medical use and the likelihood that people will abuse them. Schedule 1 drugs have little evidence of being medically useful and have a high risk for addiction. They include ecstasy, heroin, and LSD. Schedule 5 drugs have the least risk for addiction. Schedule 5 drugs include cough medicines containing codeine. The Controlled Substances Act also repealed the mandatory minimums established in 1951. In 1971, Nixon officially launched the War on Drugs. The president said drug abuse was "public enemy number one."[5] Nixon's War on Drugs included increasing government funding for drug-control agencies and suggestions for mandatory prison sentences for drug crimes.

Not long after, the fight against drugs went in a different direction. In the mid-1970s, 12 states reduced their penalties for possessing small amounts of marijuana. But in 1986, the Anti-Drug Abuse Act, passed under President Ronald Reagan, brought a renewed effort in the War on Drugs. The law had several facets, including making it easier for authorities to seize a drug offender's assets, such as money. The Anti-Drug Abuse Act also outlined mandatory minimum prison sentences for drug crimes. Possession of 35 ounces (1,000 g) of heroin or 176 ounces (5,000 g) of powder cocaine came

CLINTON'S CRIME LAW

In 1994, President Bill Clinton signed the Violent Crime Control and Law Enforcement Act into law. It was the biggest crime legislation in US history, adding 100,000 new officers to the nation's police forces and designating $9.7 billion for prisons and $6.1 billion for prevention programs. The legislation also included a variety of items pertaining to criminal law, including expansion of the federal death penalty. The legislation also created the three-strikes rule, which requires "mandatory life imprisonment without possibility of parole for federal offenders with three or more convictions for serious violent felonies or drug trafficking crimes."[6]

In July 2015, Clinton spoke about the three-strikes rule, saying there had been a "roaring decade of rising crime." He said the legislation helped create "the biggest drop in crime history." But Clinton also acknowledged, "The bad news is we had a lot of people who were essentially locked up who were minor actors for way too long."[7] In 2010, the federal prison population was 208,000. Forty-eight percent of inmates were serving time for drug crimes.[8]

with a mandatory ten-year sentence. Possession of 4 ounces (100 g) of heroin or 18 ounces (500 g) of powder cocaine resulted in a minimum of five years. And the act created harsher punishments for crack cocaine than for powder cocaine. For example, 176 ounces (5,000 g) of powder cocaine and 2 ounces (50 g) of crack cocaine resulted in the same mandatory minimum sentence: ten years.

The differences in sentences for powder and crack cocaine have had far-reaching effects based on race, with the mandatory minimum-sentencing laws considered biased against African Americans. According to a 2010 *US News and World Report* article based on sentencing statistics, "No class of drug is as racially skewed as crack in terms of number of offenses."[9] The US Sentencing Commission reported 5,669 sentences for crack in 2009. Of those, 79 percent of offenders were African American, 10 percent were Hispanic, and 10 percent were white. By contrast, the 6,020 sentences for powder cocaine had 17 percent white offenders, 28 percent African American, and 53 percent Hispanic.[10] The average time served in prison was 115 months for crack offenders and 87 months for powder cocaine offenders.[11]

The combination of African Americans being arrested more often for crack and crack resulting in longer prison sentences has contributed to a prison population that is disproportionately African American. This was evident in the early 1990s, less than ten years after the mandatory minimums were established. In 1993, African Americans accounted for 33.8 percent of the US prison population and 12.1 percent of the country's total population.[12] Twenty-five years later, the disparity still existed. In 2018, African Americans were 38.1 percent of the prison population and 13.4 percent of the total population.[13]

In 2010, President Barack Obama signed the Fair Sentencing Act into law. Its goal was to decrease the disparity in sentences for different types of cocaine created by the Anti-Drug Abuse Act. The Fair Sentencing Act increased

In 2010, President Barack Obama, *left*, and Attorney General Eric Holder shake hands at an event honoring police officers.

the possession amounts of crack cocaine needed for a mandatory minimum sentence. For example, a ten-year sentence would require possession of 10 ounces (280 g) instead of 2 ounces (50 g).

That same year, and again in 2013, the US Department of Justice also took steps to reform sentencing. Attorney General Eric Holder told federal prosecutors to be less aggressive in charging nonviolent, low-level drug crimes that have mandatory minimums. This led to a record low in 2014 of federal prosecutors seeking mandatory minimums for nonviolent drug crimes. Holder commented on the change:

> For years prior to this administration, federal prosecutors were not only encouraged—but required—to always seek the most severe prison sentence possible for all drug cases, no matter the relative risk they posed to public safety. I have made a break from that philosophy. While old habits are hard to break, these numbers show that a dramatic shift is underway in the mindset of prosecutors handling nonviolent drug offenses.[14]

However, in 2017, during President Donald Trump's administration, the Department of Justice reversed Obama's and Holder's policies. Attorney General Jeff Sessions instructed prosecutors to focus heavily on all drug crimes.

MARIJUANA

In 1970, the Controlled Substances Act made marijuana a Schedule 1 drug. In 1972, the Shafer Commission, a group Nixon established, advised the president to make marijuana legal. The Schedule 1 classification made it difficult for researchers to get marijuana for studies, which kept them from making medicines from marijuana.

Still, some Americans demanded medical marijuana, and some state legislators listened. Alaska, Maine, and Oregon decriminalized marijuana in the 1970s. By 2018, medical marijuana was legal in 31 states, and recreational marijuana was legal in nine states.[15] However, marijuana remained illegal at the federal level.

DISCUSSION STARTERS

- What do you think about criminalizing drug use? Should people go to jail for using drugs? Why or why not?
- This chapter shows how different presidents have created or changed drug policies. Which changes did you agree with or disagree with? Explain.
- Do you think mandatory minimum sentences are effective? Why or why not?

CHAPTER EIGHT

CYBERCRIMES

Cybercrimes, such as hacking, have started to happen increasingly often with advancements in technology.

Relatively recent advances in technology have resulted in new crimes. Cybercrimes rely on computer technology and the internet. They include cyberbullying, identity theft, and hacking.

States began creating computer-crime laws in the 1970s. These laws include crimes that are specifically computer related, such as hacking, which is accessing a computer or computer network illegally. For example, in 1984, Virginia passed the Virginia Computer Crimes Act. The act has been updated several times since then as technology has continued to evolve. The legislation specifies several computer crimes, including fraud, spam, trespassing, and invasion of privacy. Some of the crimes are felonies, such as committing computer fraud with a value of $200 or more.

CYBERBULLYING

One crime that has developed with advances in technology is cyberbullying. Cyberbullying is bullying via digital devices, such as computers and smartphones. Cyberbullying can happen in texts and online, such as on social media. Cyberbullying includes many actions, such as sending hurtful messages or threats to someone via email or cell phone, posting hurtful or threatening messages online, and

Cyberbullying is considered a crime in some states.

spreading rumors online or by text. In 2017, the Centers for Disease Control and Prevention reported that approximately 15 percent of high school students were estimated to have been cyberbullied in 2016.[1]

The first cyberbullying laws emerged in the mid-2000s. No federal law exists, although Linda Sanchez, a US representative from California, introduced the Megan Meier Cyberbullying Prevention Act in 2009. Sanchez named the bill after a 13-year-old who killed herself in 2006 after being cyberbullied. The House of Representatives had not voted on the bill as of early 2019.

All 50 states have bullying laws. As of November 2018, 48 states addressed cyberbullying within their bullying laws. Eighteen of these 48 states penalize cyberbullying as a crime.[2] For example, California state law specifies:

> Every person who, with intent to place another person in reasonable fear for his or her safety, or the safety of the other person's immediate family, by means of an electronic communication device . . . electronically distributes, publishes, e-mails, hyperlinks, or makes available for downloading, personal identifying information . . . or an electronic message of a harassing nature about another person . . . is guilty of a misdemeanor.[3]

SEXTING

Sexting, a combination of the words *sex* and *texting*, is sending sexually explicit images or words via text messaging. In several states, sexting is a crime if the communications involve someone younger than 18. As of 2018, six states had laws that punished some instances of sexting as felonies.[4] Additionally, when sexting occurs between an adult and a minor and involves nude photos of the minor, the adult may face a child pornography charge. If convicted, the person could face jail time and be required to register as a sex offender for life. In some states, minors have also been charged with child pornography in sexting cases.

Rather than making cyberbullying a crime addressed by the legal system, some states make the public school system responsible for disciplining students who engage in cyberbullying. And every state except Montana has within its bullying legislation a requirement that schools establish a formal policy about bullying. Requirements for these policies vary by state.

Identity theft includes stealing credit card information.

IDENTITY THEFT

Another cybercrime is identity theft, which is also a crime under the category of fraud and financial theft. Identity theft occurs when one person uses another person's personal information, such as a social security number or credit card information, to commit fraud. Thieves can steal personal information in different ways, such as by taking a person's wallet or mail. But some obtain personal information electronically.

Many companies store information about their customers electronically. Sometimes, this information ends up in the hands of the wrong people as a result of data breaches. Data breaches can occur in several ways. A company may

FIGHTING RANSOMWARE ATTACKS

Some cyber criminals use software called ransomware to take over a victim's computer, requiring the person to pay a ransom to regain control. In some cases, such criminals have targeted the computers of city offices. In March 2018, a cyberattack in Atlanta, Georgia, left thousands of city workers unable to access their computer network and kept residents from making online payments, such as for water bills. In recent years, some states have passed ransomware-specific laws, including California, Connecticut, Texas, and Wyoming. However, legal experts question the usefulness of these new laws. Andrew Sellars, a professor and director of the Technology and Cyberlaw Clinic at the Boston University School of Law, explained, "The concern is not for a need for an additional law." Rather, the concern is "getting . . . state or local-level law enforcement equipped to do computer investigation of this nature," he said.[5] Another challenge is making possession of ransomware a crime. Some experts worry that such legislation could be problematic for cybersecurity companies that use ransomware in their work, such as for testing.

mistakenly send customers' information to an unintended person or mistakenly put the information online. Sometimes, someone working at the company accesses the information intentionally, which is an insider data breach. Hacking occurs when someone accesses a computer network without permission. That is, they get electronic data illegally.

All 50 states have cybercrime legislation. Most of the laws regard accessing information without authorization, which is sometimes called computer trespass. Some states detail specific cybercrimes, such as phishing. Phishing is a scam in which one person cons another person electronically into sharing personal information. In 2005, California was the first state to establish a law focused on phishing. People convicted of phishing can be fined up to $2,500 per crime.

There is no federal law specific to phishing. The Controlling the Assault of Non-Solicited Pornography and Marketing (CAN-SPAM) Act, passed in 2003, is intended to fight spam, which is used in phishing schemes. But the law does not use the word *phishing*. Violators of this law face a fine of $250 per spam email. Politicians have introduced antiphishing legislation, but it has failed to pass into law. Neither the Anti-Phishing Act of 2004 nor the Anti-Phishing Act of 2005 became law.

Lack of specific antiphishing legislation at the federal level does not mean federal authorities are without means of fighting the crime. For example, a prosecutor could apply federal legislation regarding fraud to people who phish. Punishment varies and can include a fine and a prison sentence.

DISCUSSION STARTERS

- Do you think criminal law is adapting well to new technologies?
- Do you think cyberbullying should be addressed by criminal law? Why or why not?
- Why do you think some state lawmakers created phishing-specific laws?

CHAPTER NINE

CRIMINAL LAW AND HOMELAND SECURITY

The Transportation Security Administration (TSA), which stations officers at US airports, is part of the Department of Homeland Security.

n the twenty-first century, two areas of criminal law have
raised considerable public discussion: terrorism and
immigration. Terrorism became an especially important
topic for Americans, including lawmakers, after the terrorist
attacks of September 11, 2001. Immigration has a long history
in US legal code. But in the 2010s, it was pushed to the
forefront of national discussions, especially during the 2016
presidential election and the administration of President
Donald Trump.

THE HOMELAND SECURITY ACT

On September 11, 2001, members of the terrorist group
al-Qaeda crashed two hijacked airliners into the World Trade
Center towers in New York City. A third plane crashed into

Smoke fills the sky above New York City as the World Trade Center burns
on September 11, 2001.

the Pentagon, a government building in Washington, DC. A fourth went down in a field in Pennsylvania after passengers fought back against the hijackers. Nearly 3,000 people died in the attacks.[1]

The attack prompted President George W. Bush to sign the Homeland Security Act into law in 2002. The act addressed immigration and terrorism in a single move by creating the Department of Homeland Security (DHS). According to the website of the US Senate Committee on Homeland Security and Governmental Affairs, the act "consolidated 22 diverse agencies and bureaus into the Department of Homeland Security (DHS) with a mandate of preventing and responding to natural and man-made disasters."[2]

Many DHS agencies focus on preventing terrorism. For example, the Domestic Nuclear Detection Office works to detect nuclear weapons and dirty bombs, which are designed to contaminate a small area with radioactive material. A dirty bomb would not likely cause illness to those who are exposed. However, it would cause fear and contaminate the exposed area, which would be expensive to clean up. Other DHS agencies that focus on terrorism include the Office of Intelligence and Analysis (I&A) and the

Transportation Security Administration (TSA). I&A gathers

information with the purpose of identifying possible

threats to security on US land. TSA focuses on keeping US

transportation systems safe.

The Homeland Security Act addressed immigration

by ending the US Immigration and Naturalization Service

(INS) and moving most of its functions to the DHS. The DHS

includes Customs and Border Protection (CBP), Immigration

and Customs Enforcement (ICE), and US Citizenship and

Immigration Services (USCIS), which replaced the INS. CBP

oversees the US borders, helping conduct travel and trade

CRIMES AGAINST THE UNITED STATES

Terrorism is one of several acts that are crimes against the United States. These crimes also include espionage, rioting, sedition, and treason. Espionage, or spying, involves sharing confidential government information with people who do not have government approval to have it. A conviction can result in a life sentence. Members of the US military who are convicted of espionage may be sentenced to death.

The punishment for a federal rioting conviction is much less severe. It can include fines and up to five years in prison. Someone acquitted of a state rioting charge cannot be charged for the same acts at the federal level.

Sedition occurs when two or more people work together to try to overthrow the government, such as by encouraging violence by others. Taking US property by force is also sedition. A person who is convicted may be fined and sentenced to up to 20 years in prison.

Treason is the only crime the US Constitution specifically defines: "Treason against the United States, shall consist only in levying War against them, or in adhering to their Enemies, giving them Aid and Comfort. No Person shall be convicted of Treason unless on the Testimony of two Witnesses to the same overt Act, or on Confession in open Court."[3] Federal legislation outlines the penalty for treason as a minimum fine of $10,000 and a minimum prison sentence of five years. A conviction for treason may also carry the penalty of death.

smoothly while keeping an eye out for illegal activity, such as drug trafficking and people entering the country illegally. ICE is one of DHS's biggest agencies. After the FBI, ICE is the largest law enforcement entity in the United States. One of ICE's top roles is to keep terrorists from getting US weapons. USCIS oversees work permits and citizenship for immigrants.

TERRORISM

Even before the Homeland Security Act, there were US laws that separately addressed crimes associated with terrorism and immigration. Early US anti-terrorism laws were aimed at preventing international terrorist attacks against the United States. Current terrorism legislation has been expanded to other acts, such as helping terrorists by hiding them or giving them money.

Federal law defines international and domestic terrorism. The definitions refer to similar actions, but the difference is in location. According to federal law, international terrorism activities take place outside of the United States "or transcend national boundaries in terms of the means by which they are accomplished, the persons they appear intended to [target, or the location] in which their perpetrators operate or seek asylum."[4] By contrast, domestic terrorism happens only within the United States. All penalties for terrorism include a prison sentence. Conviction for terrorism that results in death is punishable by a maximum sentence of life in prison or death.

Several states also have laws regarding terroristic acts that occur within a single state. New Jersey's terrorism law covers many criminal acts, including murder, kidnapping, disarming a police officer, and carjacking. Terrorism is a first-degree felony in New Jersey. Conviction results in a sentence of 30 years to life in prison. Any prison sentence under that conviction includes no possibility of parole until 30 years have been served. If the terrorist act results in death, the sentence can be life in prison with no possibility of parole.

IMMIGRATION

From the late 1990s to the early 2000s, laws emerged in response to terrorism and unauthorized immigrants. This legislation focused on border patrol and made entering the country more difficult. However, millions of undocumented immigrants still live in the United States. In 2018, the BBC reported the United States had approximately 11 million undocumented immigrants.[5]

HUMAN TRAFFICKING

Human trafficking, in which victims are treated as property and are exploited in different ways, is an issue worldwide. Some people are forced into prostitution or forced to take part in sexual acts to be used in pornography. Some are forced into slavery. According to the nonprofit DoSomething.org, there are approximately 20 million to 30 million slaves around the world as a result of human trafficking. The average age of a person entering the US sex trade is 12 to 14 years old. In the United States, 14,500 to 17,500 people are victims of human trafficking each year.[6] Three of the cities with the most child sex trafficking in the United States are in California: Los Angeles, San Diego, and San Francisco. Texas and Florida have the next-highest amounts of reported human trafficking cases. The crime occurs in every state.

The United States addresses human trafficking in different laws. The Trafficking Victims Protection Act of 2000 was the first comprehensive federal law to broadly address human trafficking. It has three elements: protection, prosecution, and prevention. Sex traffickers whose victims are children can be sentenced to ten years to life in prison. In addition to paying fines and serving time, criminals have to pay restitution to their victims. And criminals lose any property involved in human trafficking.

Being in the United States illegally and entering the country illegally are not the same. An example of being in the country illegally is entering the United States through a tourist visa and staying past its expiration date. Being in the country illegally is not usually a crime. Rather, it is a civil offense that may result in deportation. However, entering the United States without the appropriate authorization is a federal crime. US immigration laws specify the crimes of entering the United States in places other than designated entry points, avoiding examination by immigration agents, and helping other people enter the country illegally. Marriage fraud, which is marrying someone to avoid the immigration laws, is also a crime.

Punishment for a first offense of illegal entry includes a fine of $50 to $250, jail time of not more than six months, or both a fine and jail time. If a person is caught entering the country illegally a second time, the possible fine is $100 to $500 and possible jail time is up to two years. People found guilty of marriage fraud face a fine of up to $250,000, a prison sentence of up to five years, or both.

Between 1990 and 2010, the crimes prosecuted most often in US federal courts had to do with immigration. But statistics show something more. The government has

ICE, which is the agency responsible for arresting undocumented immigrants, was created as part of the Homeland Security Act.

used criminal offenses to influence immigration. Between 1997 and 2009, the United States deported nearly 900,000 immigrants because they had criminal convictions.[7] Some of these immigrants had been living in the United States legally and for many years. And most of the convictions were for minor, nonviolent offenses. In a 2010 ruling on a case involving immigration and criminal charges, the US Supreme Court commented on this convergence of criminal and immigration law:

> The landscape of federal immigration law has changed dramatically. . . . While once there was only a narrow class of deportable [criminal] offenses and judges wielded broad discretionary authority to prevent deportation, immigration reforms over time have expanded the class of deportable offenses and limited the authority of judges to alleviate the harsh consequences of deportation. The "drastic measure" of deportation . . . is now virtually inevitable for a vast number of noncitizens convicted of crimes.[8]

Almost ten years later, this focus on immigration and criminal activity continues. Under the Trump administration, ICE has increased its efforts to arrest undocumented immigrants. In 2018, ICE arrested 158,581 undocumented immigrants. This was an increase of 11 percent over 2017.[9]

Amid heated national discussion over immigration during the Trump administration, some people have advocated for abolishing ICE because of the way the agency has increasingly targeted all undocumented immigrants. Still, other Americans support the crackdown on immigration.

ICE has sought out all undocumented workers and made its first goal to arrest and deport those undocumented immigrants who have been convicted of a crime. Sixty-five percent of the undocumented workers ICE arrested in 2018 had been convicted of a crime. More than 50 percent of those convictions were for driving drunk. And 16 percent of the charges and convictions against the arrested immigrants were related to immigration.[10]

President Trump has pushed the government to focus more on immigration. He promoted immigration reform while campaigning for the 2016 election and continued that stance after taking office. He regularly depicts immigrants from south of the United States as criminals. To this effect, he has highlighted crimes committed by undocumented immigrants. With that, he advocates for creating stricter immigration legislation and for building a wall along the US-Mexico border. Trump's public comments on the subject have fueled heated national conversation about the topic of illegal immigration and the ways in which it can be associated with crime.

US criminal law is complex and detailed. It has evolved with the nation, reflecting changes in society, technology, and the beliefs of legislators. It is fluid and will continue to change, building upon the foundation lawmakers have created and adding to the nation's long history of criminal law.

DISCUSSION STARTERS

- Do you think the Homeland Security Act was a helpful response to the September 11 terrorist attacks? Explain.
- Why do you think US criminal law addresses domestic terrorism and international terrorism separately?
- Do you think immigration and criminal law should be related? Explain.

ESSENTIAL FACTS

SIGNIFICANT EVENTS

- In 1976, Nebraska became the first state to make spousal rape a crime. By 1993, all 50 states had made spousal rape a crime.

- In 1986, the Anti-Drug Abuse Act outlined mandatory minimum prison sentences for drug crimes. This disproportionately affected African Americans and created racial disparity in the country's prison population.

- In 1994, the Violent Crime Control and Law Enforcement Act created the three-strikes rule, making a life sentence mandatory for federal offenders with three or more convictions for drug trafficking or serious violent felonies.

- In 1994, the Jacob Wetterling Act established a national sex offender registry in the United States.

- In 2009, new federal legislation broadened the nation's definition of hate crimes to include crimes based on disability, gender identity, or sexual orientation.

KEY PLAYERS

- President Richard M. Nixon focused heavily on drug crime, first by signing the Controlled Substances Act into law in 1970, then by declaring the War on Drugs in 1971.

- President Bill Clinton signed the Violent Crime Control and Law Enforcement Act into law in 1994, creating the three-strikes rule.

- President George W. Bush signed the Homeland Security Act of 2002, creating the Department of Homeland Security.

- President Barack Obama signed the Fair Sentencing Act into law in 2010, seeking to decrease the racial disparity in sentences for different types of cocaine.

- President Donald Trump sought to crack down on undocumented immigration in 2017 and 2018, leading to numerous arrests.

IMPACT ON SOCIETY

Criminal laws are meant to deter people from committing crimes and to bring justice for victims of crimes. Laws develop and change to reflect changes in societal attitudes and social norms. Some laws emerge as a result of advances in technology. Laws also develop in response to events and because of lawmakers' beliefs.

Penalties in criminal law change the lives of many who are convicted. Incarceration can take away a person's physical freedom for decades and cause felony convicts to lose a variety of rights. In some instances, a conviction can result in the death penalty. Some laws have a racial bias and have led to disproportionate numbers of people of color being penalized and imprisoned.

QUOTE

"They had bad judgment, but they didn't commit a murder—and when I understood this, I knew we had to fix that."

—*California state senator Nancy Skinner, on changing the state's law regarding the crime of felony murder*

GLOSSARY

amendment
A formal addition or change to a document or law.

arson
The illegal act of intentionally setting fire to a building or other structure.

civil law
Law that applies to private rights and is not punishable by incarceration.

codeine
A drug developed from opium used in cough medicine.

criminalize
To make something illegal.

decriminalize
To make a crime a lesser offense or to no longer consider a specific action a crime.

defendant
A person accused of a crime who has had a legal charge made against him or her.

exploit
To use, typically in a harmful way.

fraud
Illegal deception with the goal of making money.

jurisdiction
A certain area within which a group has authority to make a legal decision or take legal action.

life sentence
A sentence for a crime that requires people to be imprisoned for the rest of their natural life.

mediation

The process of negotiating, or working out differences, with the help of an impartial, or unbiased, person.

naturalization

The process of obtaining citizenship.

opiate

A drug containing or made from opium, such as codeine or morphine, that usually causes drowsiness and relieves pain.

probation

The release of a prisoner who remains under supervision instead of incarceration.

prosecutors

Legal officials who charge people with criminal offenses and argue for the charges in court.

restitution

Money paid for injury or loss.

spam

Unwanted messages and texts; electronic junk mail.

sue

To take someone to court for violation of civil law.

trespass

To go onto someone's property without that person's permission.

ADDITIONAL RESOURCES

SELECTED BIBLIOGRAPHY

Cohn, D'Vera. "How US Immigration Laws and Rules Have Changed through History." *Pew Research Center*, 30 Sept. 2015, pewresearch.org. Accessed 11 Nov. 2018.

"Criminal Charges." *FindLaw*. Thomson Reuters, 2018. 12 Nov. 2018.

Kurtzleben, Danielle. "Data Show Racial Disparity in Crack Sentencing." *U.S. News & World Report*, 3 Aug. 2010, usnews.com.

FURTHER READINGS

Harris, Duchess, and Carla Mooney. *The Juvenile Justice System*. Abdo, 2020.

Harris, Duchess, and Rebecca Morris. *The History of Law Enforcement*. Abdo, 2020.

Lippman, Matthew. *Essential Criminal Law*. Sage, 2017.

ONLINE RESOURCES

To learn more about the history of criminal law, visit **abdobooklinks.com** or scan this QR code. These links are routinely monitored and updated to provide the most current information available.

MORE INFORMATION

For more information on this subject, contact or visit the following organizations:

Alcatraz East Crime Museum
2757 Parkway
Pigeon Forge, TN 37863
865-453-3278
alcatrazeast.com

The museum offers permanent and temporary exhibits focused on crime and law enforcement and has a crime library that offers information online.

Youth Law Center
832 Folsom Street, #700
San Francisco, CA 94107
415-543-3379
ylc.org

The Youth Law Center (YLC) advocates for children in foster care and the juvenile justice system, including in court, through public education, and by working to reform policies.

SOURCE NOTES

CHAPTER 1. THE JACOB WETTERLING ACT

1. "Timeline of the Wetterling Investigation." *St. Cloud Times*, 26 Sept. 2016, sctimes.com. Accessed 6 Mar. 2019.

2. Pam Louwagie and Jennifer Brooks. "Danny Heinrich Confesses to Abducting and Killing Jacob Wetterling." *Star Tribune*, 7 Sept. 2016, startribune.com. Accessed 6 Mar. 2019.

3. Louwagie and Brooks, "Danny Heinrich Confesses to Abducting and Killing Jacob Wetterling."

4. "About the MN Predatory Offender Unit." *Minnesota Predatory Offender Registration*, 2010, por.state.mn.us. Accessed 6 Mar. 2019.

CHAPTER 2. CRIMINAL LAW BASICS

1. Brian Duignan. "What Is the Difference between Criminal Law and Civil Law?" *Encyclopædia Britannica*, 2018, britannica.com. Accessed 6 Mar. 2019.

2. "Code of Hammurabi." *History.com*, 9 Nov. 2009, history.com. Accessed 6 Mar. 2019.

3. "Frequently Asked Questions." *US Department of the Interior, Bureau of Indian Affairs*, bia.gov. Accessed 6 Mar. 2019.

4. "Felon Voting Rights." *National Conference of State Legislatures*, 21 Dec. 2018, ncsl.org. Accessed 6 Mar. 2019.

CHAPTER 3. CRIMES AGAINST A PERSON

1. "Domestic Violence." *Encyclopedia.com*, 2002, encyclopedia.com. Accessed 13 Mar. 2019.

2. "Violence Against Women Act (VAWA) Reauthorization 2013." *US Department of Justice*, 26 Mar. 2015, justice.gov. Accessed 6 Mar. 2019.

CHAPTER 4. MURDER AND MANSLAUGHTER

1. "2016 Crime Statistics Released." *FBI News*, 25 Sept. 2017, fbi.gov/news. Accessed 6 Mar. 2019.

2. "Facts about the Death Penalty." *Death Penalty Information Center*, 12 Mar. 2019, deathpenaltyinfo.org. Accessed 13 Mar. 2019.

3. "Mens Rea." *Cornell Law School Legal Information Institute*, n.d., law.cornell.edu. Accessed 6 Mar. 2019.

4. "30 States with the Death Penalty and 20 States with Death Penalty Bans." *ProCon.org*, 16 Oct. 2018, procon.org. Accessed 6 Mar. 2019.

5. "Vehicular Homicide." *Justia*, n.d., justia.com. Accessed 6 Mar. 2019.

6. Abbie VanSickle. "Can It Be Murder If You Didn't Kill Anyone?" *Marshall Project*, 27 June 2018, themarshallproject.org. Accessed 6 Mar. 2019.

7. VanSickle, "Can It Be Murder If You Didn't Kill Anyone?"

8. Alexei Koseff. "Hundreds Serving Time for Murder Could Get Sprung under New California Law." *Sacramento Bee*, 30 Sept. 2018, sacbee.com. Accessed 6 Mar. 2019.

9. Koseff, "Hundreds Serving Time for Murder Could Get Sprung under New California Law."

10. Koseff, "Hundreds Serving Time for Murder Could Get Sprung under New California Law."

11. "Bernhard Goetz." *Biography.com*, 2 Apr. 2014, biography.com. Accessed 6 Mar. 2019.

CHAPTER 5. SEX CRIMES

1. "Rape." *FindLaw*, n.d., criminal.findlaw.com. Accessed 6 Mar. 2019.

2. "2016 Crime Statistics Released." *FBI News*, 25 Sept. 2017, fbi.gov/news. Accessed 6 Mar. 2019.

3. Laura Santhanam. "Why Do State Laws Put an Expiration Date on Sex Crimes?" *PBS NewsHour*, 28 Nov. 2017, pbs.org. Accessed 6 Mar. 2019.

4. "State by State Guide on Statutes of Limitations." *RAINN*, n.d., rainn.org. Accessed 6 Mar. 2019.

5. "An Updated Definition of Rape." *US Department of Justice*, 6 Jan. 2012, justice.gov. Accessed 6 Mar. 2019.

CHAPTER 6. PROPERTY CRIMES

1. "2016 Crime Statistics Released." *FBI News*, 25 Sept. 2017, fbi.gov/news. Accessed 6 Mar. 2019.

2. Jared Keller. "The Ongoing Destruction of Black Churches." *Pacific Standard*, 7 July 2015, psmag.com. Accessed 6 Mar. 2019.

3. "Arson." *Encyclopedia.com*, 2005, encyclopedia.com. Accessed 6 Mar. 2019.

4. John S. Hausman. "Michigan's Arson Laws Getting Stricter, More Specific." *MLive*, 2 Apr. 2013, mlive.com. Accessed 6 Mar. 2019.

5. "2016 Crime Statistics Released."

6. "The Effects of Changing Felony Theft Thresholds." *PEW*, 12 Apr. 2017, pewtrusts.org. Accessed 6 Mar. 2019.

7. "What Are Your Miranda Rights?" *MirandaWarning.org*, n.d., mirandawarning.org. Accessed 6 Mar. 2019.

8. "The Effects of Changing Felony Theft Thresholds."

9. "White-Collar Crime." *Cornell Law School Legal Information Institute*, n.d., law.cornell.edu. Accessed 6 Mar. 2019.

SOURCE NOTES CONTINUED

CHAPTER 7. DRUG CRIMES

1. "New FBI Report Shows Drug Arrests Increased in 2016, as Drug War Rages On." *Drug Policy Alliance*, 25 Sept. 2017, drugpolicy.org. Accessed 6 Mar. 2019.

2. "New FBI Report Shows Drug Arrests Increased in 2016, as Drug War Rages On."

3. "Mandatory Minimums and Sentencing Reform." *Criminal Justice Policy Foundation*, n.d., cjpf.org. Accessed 6 Mar. 2019.

4. "War on Drugs." *History.com*, 31 May 2017, history.com. Accessed 6 Mar. 2019.

5. "War on Drugs."

6. "Violence Crime Control and Law Enforcement Act of 1994 Fact Sheet." *National Criminal Justice Reference Service*, 24 Oct. 1994, ncjrs.gov. Accessed 6 Mar. 2019.

7. "Bill Clinton Regrets 'Three Strikes' Bill." *BBC*, 16 July 2015, bbc.com. Accessed 6 Mar. 2019.

8. "Bill Clinton Regrets 'Three Strikes' Bill."

9. Danielle Kurtzleben. "Data Show Racial Disparity in Crack Sentencing." *U.S. News & World Report*, 3 Aug. 2010, usnews.com. Accessed 6 Mar. 2019.

10. Kurtzleben, "Data Show Racial Disparity in Crack Sentencing."

11. Kurtzleben, "Data Show Racial Disparity in Crack Sentencing."

12. Marvin D. Free Jr. "The Impact of Federal Sentencing Reforms on African Americans." *Journal of Black Studies*, vol. 28, no. 2, Nov. 1997. 268.

13. "Inmate Race." *Federal Bureau of Prisons*, 26 Jan. 2019, bop.gov. Accessed 6 Mar. 2019.

14. "In Milestone for Sentencing Reform, Attorney General Holder Announces Record Reduction in Mandatory Minimums against Nonviolent Drug Offenders." *US Department of Justice*, 17 Feb. 2015, justice.gov. Accessed 6 Mar. 2019.

15. Jeremy Berke and Skye Gould. "This Map Shows Every US State Where Pot Is Legal." *Business Insider*, 4 Jan. 2019, businessinsider.com. Accessed 6 Mar. 2019.

CHAPTER 8. CYBERCRIMES

1. "What Is Cyberbullying." *StopBullying.gov*, n.d., stopbullying.gov. Accessed 6 Mar. 2019.

2. Sameer Hinduja and Justin W. Patchin. "State Bullying Laws." *Cyberbullying Research Center*, Nov. 2018, cyberbullying.org. Accessed 13 Mar. 2019.

3. "Bullying Laws in California." *Cyberbullying Research Center*, n.d., cyberbullying.org. Accessed 6 Mar. 2019.

4. Sameer Hinduja and Justin W. Patchin. "State Sexting Laws." *Cyberbullying Research Center*, Nov. 2018, cyberbullying.org. Accessed 13 Mar. 2019.

5. Alan Neuhauser. "Can the Law Stop Ransomware?" *U.S. News & World Report*, 13 Apr. 2018, usnews.com. Accessed 6 Mar. 2019.

CHAPTER 9. CRIMINAL LAW AND HOMELAND SECURITY

1. "9/11 Attacks." *History.com*, 17 Feb. 2010, history.com. Accessed 6 Mar. 2019.

2. "Homeland Security." *US Senate Committee on Homeland Security & Governmental Affairs*, n.d., hsgac.senate.gov. Accessed 6 Mar. 2019.

3. "Treason." *FindLaw,* n.d., criminal.findlaw.com. Accessed 6 Mar. 2019.

4. "18 US Code § 2331. Definitions." *Cornell Law School Legal Information Institute*, n.d., law.cornell.edu. Accessed 6 Mar. 2019.

5. "Are All Undocumented Immigrants Criminals?" *BBC*, 22 July 2018, bbc.com. Accessed 6 Mar. 2019.

6. "11 Facts about Human Trafficking." *DoSomething.org*, n.d., dosomething.org. Accessed 6 Mar. 2019.

7. Allegra M. McLeod. "The U.S. Criminal-Immigration Convergence and Its Possible Undoing." *American Criminal Law Review*, vol. 49, no. 1, 2012. 107–108.

8. McLeod, "The U.S. Criminal-Immigration Convergence and Its Possible Undoing," 108.

9. David Shortell. "ICE Arrests Continue to Rise in Trump's Second Year." *CNN*, 14 Dec. 2018, cnn.com. Accessed 6 Mar. 2019.

10. Shortell, "ICE Arrests Continue to Rise in Trump's Second Year."

INDEX

Madigan, Lisa, 52
Madoff, Bernie, 69
mandatory minimum sentencing, 73–79
manslaughter, 40–41, 43–44
marijuana, 73–75, 79
Michigan, 62
Minnesota, 6–12, 55
Miranda rights, 65
misdemeanors, 19–21, 32–33, 45, 47, 56, 60, 64, 84
murder, 10, 16, 21, 31, 34, 40–42, 45–47, 94

National Center for Missing and Exploited Children, 11
New Jersey, 94
New York, 21, 42, 44, 47, 51–52, 90
Nixon, Richard, 74–75, 79
nuclear weapons, 91

Obama, Barack, 77–78
Ohio, 21

parole, 22–23, 24, 75, 94
plea bargaining, 10
probation, 20, 22–23, 24, 64, 66

rape, 21, 37, 42–43, 50–55
Reagan, Ronald, 75
robbery, 29, 42, 45, 60

Schaeffer, Rebecca, 33–34
September 11, 2001, 90–91
Sessions, Jeff, 78
sex offenders, 11–12, 56–57, 84
sexual assault, 8–10, 37, 50, 52–55
Sherman Antitrust Act, 68
Skinner, Nancy, 45–47
stalking, 28, 32–34, 36–37

theft, 31, 42, 60, 63–66, 69, 82, 85
Transportation Security Administration (TSA), 92
treason, 42, 92
Trump, Donald, 78, 90, 97–99

vandalism, 21, 32, 35, 60
vehicular homicide, 43–45
Violence Against Women Act (VAWA), 36–37
Violent Crime Control and Law Enforcement Act, 34, 74
Virginia, 24, 42, 54, 82

War on Drugs, 72, 74–75
Wetterling, Jacob, 6–12
Wetterling, Patty, 8, 10–11
white-collar crime, 67–69

ABOUT THE AUTHORS

DUCHESS HARRIS, JD, PHD

Dr. Harris is a professor of American Studies at Macalester College and curator of the Duchess Harris Collection of ABDO books. She is also the coauthor of the titles in the collection, which features popular selections such as *Hidden Human Computers: The Black Women of NASA* and series including News Literacy and Being Female in America.

Before working with ABDO, Dr. Harris authored several other books on the topics of race, culture, and American history. She served as an associate editor for *Litigation News*, the American Bar Association Section of Litigation's quarterly flagship publication, and was the first editor in chief of *Law Raza*, an interactive online journal covering race and the law, published at William Mitchell College of Law. She has earned a PhD in American Studies from the University of Minnesota and a JD from William Mitchell College of Law.

REBECCA ROWELL

Rebecca Rowell has put her degree in publishing and writing to work as an editor and as an author, working on dozens of books. Recent topics as an author include the American middle class and the Paris climate agreement. She lives in Minneapolis, Minnesota.